THE WAY OUT

30 DEVOTIONS ON TEMPTATION AND SELF-CONTROL

Published by LifeWay Press®

ISBN 978-1-0877-4241-0
Item 005831550
Dewey Decimal Classification Number: 242
Subject Heading: DEVOTIONAL LITERATURE / BIBLE STUDY AND TEACHING / GOD

Printed in the United States of America

Student Ministry Publishing
LifeWay Resources
One LifeWay Plaza
Nashville, Tennessee 37234

We believe that the Bible has God for its author; salvation for its end; and truth, without any mixture of error, for its matter and that all Scripture is totally true and trustworthy. To review LifeWay's doctrinal guideline, please visit www.lifeway.com/doctrinalguideline.

Unless otherwise noted, all Scripture quotations are taken from the Christian Standard Bible®, Copyright © 2017 by Holman Bible Publishers. Used by permission. Christian Standard Bible® and CSB® are federally registered trademarks of Holman Bible Publishers.

publishing team

Director, Student Ministry
Ben Trueblood

Manager, Student Ministry Publishing
John Paul Basham

Editorial Team Leader
Karen Daniel

Content Editor
Kyle Wiltshire

Production Editor
Brooke Hill

Graphic Designer
Kaitlin Redmond

table of contents

intro

From the kitchen you hear your mother's voice saying, "It's time for dinner." You look down at your controller and grimace. You know that if you get 10 more XP's, you'll level up. "One more minute, Mom," you say. Ten minutes later, you hear her voice again, slightly agitated, saying, "The food is getting cold." This time, you're in the middle of a boss battle. If you defeat this one, you get a new skin. You respond, "Ok, I'm almost done." Ten minutes later, she's in full-on rage mode, hollering, "I am not going to tell you again. It's dinner time, turn that game off and come to the table RIGHT NOW!" Why is it so hard to put that controller down?

An over-indulgence in anything isn't healthy. It's not good for your heart, your soul, or your mind. But the truth is that some things just feel really tough to control. Some of our obsessions are more dangerous than others. While video games are fun, when you go over the top, spending hour upon hour racking up XPs and defeating bosses, you lose opportunities to do more constructive and productive things. In a worse case scenario, the silly little game might turn into an obsession that takes you down a path you never saw coming.

Every single person on this earth struggles with self-control in some area. While we may not all struggle with the same issues or to the same extent, there is one solution for us all. When you trust in Jesus as Savior, you receive the Holy Spirit. He helps you to remember what God has taught you and do what Scripture commands (Luke 12:12; John 14:26). A major indicator of the Holy Spirit's presence in our life is the fruit of the Spirit—one of which is self-control.

As we walk through this devotional over the next 30 days, we'll study Scripture that teaches why self-control is important, what role it plays in revealing our identity, how Satan tempts us, what to do when we feel tempted, and how to live godly, self-controlled lives.

These devotions will challenge you. They will push you to examine your life, your heart, and lean heavily on the Holy Spirit's presence in your life. When you feel discouraged, remember that He is with you every step of the way. No matter how many times you fail, God's graces always awaits you on the other side.

getting started

This devotional contains 30 days of content, broken down into sections that answer a specific question about self-control. Each day is broken down into three elements—discover, delight, and display—to help you answer core questions related to Scripture.

discover

This section helps you examine the passage in light of who God is and determine what it says about your identity in relationship to Him. Included here is the key passage and focus Scripture, along with illustrations and commentary to guide you as you study.

delight

In this section, you'll be challenged by questions and activities that help you see how God is alive and active in every detail of His Word and your life. You'll be guided to ask yourself about what the passage means for your relationship with God.

display

Here's where you really take action. Display calls you to apply what you've learned through each day's study.

prayer

Each day also includes a prayer activity in one of the three main sections.

Throughout the devotional, you'll also find extra articles and activities to help you connect with the topic personally, such as Scripture memory verses, additional resources, and quotes from leading Christian voices.

day 1

BRAND NEW FERRARI

discover|

READ 1 CORINTHIANS 6:19-20.

Don't you know that your body is a temple of the Holy Spirit who is in you, whom you have from God? You are not your own, for you were bought at a price. So glorify God with your body.

Imagine your father gave you a 2021 Ferrari Portofino M, with a 3.9-liter, turbocharged, 612 horsepower, V-8 engine. Its retail price is $244,000. He paid full price for it and entrusted it to you. It's the only one you will ever be given. How would you care for this car? Would you take it joy riding with your buddies, or would you keep it covered in the garage, barely even allowing anyone else to lay a finger on it?

When Paul wrote 1 Corinthians, his audience thought the temple in Jerusalem was where God's direct presence dwelled. In the Scripture for today, he was helping them grasp that, as believers, the Holy Spirit now indwelled within them. This is why Paul called their bodies a temple of the Holy Spirit.

Put these two ideas together. You are more valuable than a new Ferrari because the price it cost God to purchase you was His Son, Jesus. Therefore, you are not your own; you belong to Him. Now the Holy Spirit lives in you, making you a temple. The presence of the Holy Spirit fundamentally changes you. The very Spirit of God lives within you, and His presence in your life produces fruit. One aspect of that fruit of the Spirit is self-control.

delight |

How does knowing that the Holy Spirit has come to live inside you help you practice self-control?

What is the connection between Christ's work on the cross and the price mentioned in verse 20?

display |

All people are made in the image of God. That is incredible. Our bodies already have such incredible value, but when we are filled with the Holy Spirit and grasp the price Jesus paid on the cross to redeem us, we get a better idea of just how valuable we are to God. We represent more than ourselves. We represent Him.

Use pages 16-17 to memorize 1 Corinthians 6:19-20. Meditate on it and internalize it, listening carefully to the Holy Spirit's conviction for ways in which you are not glorifying God with your body. Remember always Whose you are and take whatever drastic measures are necessary to turn away from sin. Take care of your Ferrari, because your Father who loves you paid the ultimate price for it, and it's the only one you'll ever get.

Confess to God ways in which you have failed to glorify Him with your body. Thank Him for His forgiveness and for His presence within you. Ask Him to help you practice self-control and commit your body to His glory today.

day 2

THE COMPASS OF YOUR MIND

discover |

> Ask God to direct the compass of your mind. Confess if you have been entangled in the things of this world, like meaningless material pursuits, fleeting popularity, or desiring acceptance from those who do not know Christ. Ask God to set your mind's compass toward Him.

READ ROMANS 8:5-6.

For those who live according to the flesh have their minds set on the things of the flesh, but those who live according to the Spirit have their minds set on the things of the Spirit. Now the mindset of the flesh is death, but the mindset of the Spirit is life and peace.

Imagine a compass. No matter what direction you face, the compass always lets you know which way is north. The Holy Spirit in you is acting like a compass pointing you to north. No matter which way you face, He is showing you the right way to go. So, which direction are you currently facing? What occupies most of your thoughts and time? Are you living according to the flesh or the Spirit?

Dwell on the final three words of verse 6— "life and peace." Sounds amazing, right? In the Spirit, you find elusive peace that all the things of this world can never bring you. When sin is fully grown, it gives birth to death (James 1:15). That is the ultimate wage we pay in return for living according to the flesh. The the wages of our sin is death, but God's gift is eternal life (Rom. 6:23). So, does the compass of your mind currently point to death or life?

delight |

This text is more than a call to stop doing sinful things. What is it calling us to focus on instead?

What is the benefit to a Christian whose mind is set on things of the Spirit (v. 5)?

display |

We tend to hit what we are aiming at, and if you have been aiming at fleeting pleasures, you've probably hit them. But if this is the case, you are aiming at the wrong target.

Take a running catalogue throughout the day of your thoughts. Journal them as they come to you. Keep a running tally according to categories of the flesh versus the Spirit. Consider keeping a running estimate of the number of minutes or hours spent thinking of ways you can gratify what your sin nature craves versus the number of minutes or hours spent focusing on the compass of God's Spirit. At the end of the day, take inventory and be brutally honest with yourself based on what you see. Is your mindset focused on the flesh or the spirit?

day 3

NO SUPERHEROES

discover |

READ ROMANS 7:18-25.

For I know that nothing good lives in me, that is, in my flesh. For the desire to do what is good is with me, but there is no ability to do it. –Romans 7:18

There are no spiritual superheroes. Even your pastor faces temptation. No one is born exempt. Even Jesus faced the same temptations we face but was without sin (Heb. 4:15-16). The struggle you experience between Spirit enabled self-control and the sinful nature that still resides inside you is the same struggle faced by every Christian of every generation. So, take heart; you are not alone. And there is beauty in the struggle— honor in the fact that you wrestle with sin rather than just give into it every time and feel no conviction.

As Paul made clear in today's Scripture, we cannot do any good on our own. It is only by the indwelling of the Holy Spirit (the Holy Spirit living within us) that our ability to control ourselves—through supernatural means— comes about. We can take no credit for the transformation that took place in us the day we were saved, or the glorification awaiting us when we arrive in heaven. This meantime is where we experience something called "sanctification"— where the Spirit continually makes us more like Christ and less like our former, sinful selves, until our time struggling on earth is done.

delight |

In Romans 7, Paul described the struggle between his mind's desire to obey God and his flesh's constant leaning toward sin. How have you experienced this struggle in your own life?

If we had the ability to just do enough good works to save ourselves, would the cross have been necessary? Why not?

> Imitate Paul's honest humility in Romans 7 and speak with God about how your flesh just wants to sin. Then, just as Jesus demonstrated in the Lord's Prayer (Matt. 6:9-13), ask God to not bring you to temptation, but to deliver you from the evil one. Pray for the Holy Spirit's presence within you to give you self-control over the flesh.

display |

It is okay that you were not born with superpowers to avoid sin. It sets your story up so that Jesus is the Hero instead of you. Just like Paul explained in Romans 7, the struggle with your sin nature all the days of your life causes you to understand your need for a savior. If you have not yet come to terms with your own sin nature, take the Superman "S" off of your chest and be honest with God. As you ask Him for Help, He will give you self-control, among other gifts.

List three good things God has done through you lately in bullet-point form. Then, next to each of these good things, write the words, "God gets the credit for this."

day 4

BROKEN-DOWN WALL

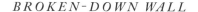

discover |

READ PROVERBS 25:28.

A person who does not control his temper is like a city whose wall is broken down.

Just about every sport has an element of defense. The object of defense is to keep the opponent from scoring or achieving their goal as a team. If there was no defense, there really wouldn't be a competition, and the sport would be boring to watch or play.

In the ancient world, the way a city defended itself was with a wall. Without a wall to protect them from intruders, a city was vulnerable to attack. Just like in sports and in the ancient world, we have to defend ourselves from attack as well. Not with self-defense classes or some type of body shield, but with self-control. The Scripture for today reminded us that when we lose our temper, we are as vulnerable to attack as an ancient city without a wall.

There is a difference between being angry and sinning. In fact, the apostle Paul wrote in Ephesians 4:26, "Be angry and do not sin." This reveals that feeling emotions of anger is not wrong—but blowing up on someone and losing our cool is. One way to maintain our walls of defense against attacks from the enemy is to practice self-control when we are tempted to lose our temper.

delight |

Why is it important to have self-control over your temper?

In what ways does an uncontrolled temper cause us to be vulnerable to the enemy's attacks?

display |

Take inventory of your relationships. Are there any you have damaged due to a lack of self-control when it comes to your temper? Invite the Holy Spirit to rebuild this broken-down wall in your life. He loves you in your broken state. He wants your voice to be taken seriously when you speak the gospel, so for His sake, invite the Holy Spirit to take over your temper both in-person and online. Seek to mend any broken relationships.

List some healthy outlets for how to express anger. Translate your frustration into energy spent on something that makes you better. These outlets could be artistic, athletic, meditating on Scripture, or worshipful.

TAKE THE PLUNGE

discover |

Therefore, brothers and sisters, in view of the mercies of God, I urge you to present your bodies as a living sacrifice, holy and pleasing to God; this is your true worship. Do not be conformed to this age, but be transformed by the renewing of your mind, so that you may discern what is the good, pleasing, and perfect will of God.

Have you ever been skiing or snowboarding down a black diamond slope? The scariest part is approaching the ledge at the top of the lift where the earth seems to drop off into nothing but sky. Today's Scripture is like making it to the peak of a black diamond slope and building up your courage to leave the lift chair, ignoring the laws of gravity, and descending the mountain.

Romans 1-11 contains some of the deepest theology ever written. Then, chapter 12 begins with "Therefore." This means that in light of all that deep theology, here's what you need to actually do. What Paul told the Romans—and us— to do was to take that leap and worshipfully head down the mountain of self-sacrifice.

Instead of being slaughtered like the Passover lambs of the Old Testament, we are to present our bodies "as a living sacrifice." Taking this plunge means we won't be like everyone else. It means we'll allow God to transform us into someone new and to renew our minds. When we do this, we'll engage in a worship that is true and leads us to discern God's will. Like skiing or snowboarding a black diamond slope, it's scary, but awesome!

delight |

How does God's mercy (v. 1) lead us to worship?

How does becoming a living sacrifice lead us to self-control?

display |

Self-sacrifice, which leads to self-control, is completely foreign to the secular culture around you. Living your life seeking God's perfect will is going to make you different from others. You have to be comfortable being out of place. Worship helps you test and discern God's will for your life because it focuses your heart on Him and not on yourself. In that state you can see His truth. Gossip, clothes, social media, popularity, and cultural acceptance fade away. Your mind is transformed and renewed when you worship.

Take the plunge into a moment of worship today. Close your eyes, get on your knees, lift your hands, do whatever you feel led to do to express your desire to worship God. Write down one insight He gave you during this time of worship below:

Sacrifice your plans, worldly desires, and ambitions on the altar of worship. Ask God to transform you with a renewed mind whereby you see the world closer to the way He does today.

"Don't you know that your body is a temple of the Holy Spirit who is in you, whom you have from God?

You are not your own, for you were bought at a price. So glorify God with your body."

I CORINTHIANS 6:19-20

day 6

YOUR HOLY CALLING

discover

> Ask the Holy Spirit to bring conviction to your heart
> regarding your conduct. Be specific when you do. Ask Him
> to teach you self-control in the pursuit of holiness today.

READ 1 PETER 1:14-16.

As obedient children, do not be conformed to the desires of your former ignorance.
But as the one who called you is holy, you also are to be holy in all your conduct;
for it is written, "Be holy, because I am holy."

It takes audacity to tell others, "Be like me." However, when that audacity is matched with perfection, there is not room to argue. To be holy is to be set apart, different, and above the things of this world. God alone is perfect in His holiness, and He has called you to be like Him.

If you have a rocky relationship with your biological father, this command might be hard to swallow. But your Heavenly Father is not your earthly father. Your Heavenly Father is perfect. As you grow to know Him, you will see this to be true and learn to trust Him more and more.

As a believer, you are His child. This is why Jesus taught us when we pray to address Him as "Our Father" (Matt. 6:9-13). So, it is our calling as Christians to obey Him and to not live in the ignorance of our former selves. The word "ignorance" (v. 14) is not an insult; it's simply a lack of knowledge. Now that we know Him, we can trust Him and seek to obey His calling to holiness in our conduct and to exercise self-control.

---

delight |

Why is it so challenging to be holy in all our conduct, as we are instructed to do in verse 15?

Why is holiness incompatible with total acceptance from the world?

display |

List a temptation that does not lead to holiness, then list an alternate activity that would help you avoid or resist the temptation. Today's text calls you to be holy in all your conduct. Choose holiness and self-control instead of sin.

SHACKLES FALL

discover |

> Ask God to remind you of the freedom He has granted you in Jesus. Be reminded that Jesus died for you so that you could be set free from sin and death.

READ 2 PETER 1:3-11.

His divine power has given us everything required for life and godliness through the knowledge of him who called us by his own glory and goodness. By these he has given us very great and precious promises, so that through them you may share in the divine nature, escaping the corruption that is in the world because of evil desire. –2 Peter 1:3–4

Imagine you were just set free from being in prison. Standing outside your cell, rubbing your wrists where the shackles scabbed them, squinting in the approaching light, you begin to feel the excitement of being free. As a follower of Christ, you have escaped sin's prison cell and have been fully equipped for what is next. The gospel is all for God's own glory, but it includes a glorious promise of freedom from sin for us.

In verses 5 and 6, Peter wrote, "For this very reason, make every effort to supplement your faith with goodness, goodness with knowledge, knowledge with self-control, self-control with endurance, endurance with godliness." Notice how he drew a line from faith to self-control. By Christ's power, we are fully equipped to live godly lives. We have no excuses. We are no longer imprisoned by our sin nature and the corruption of the world, but have been set free!

delight |

How does evil desire, or a lack of self-control, cause corruption?

List some of the great and precious promises referred to in verse 4.

display |

The promise of the gospel is salvation for sinners and glory for God, whose divine power makes it possible. Through the power of the Holy Spirit who lives in you, seek to transcend the bonds of your former sin, escaping the lie that you have no choice but to sin, and accept the calling to freedom Christ offers.

Think about if you have been making excuses for continued sin in your life. Confess to God any ways in which you have been excusing sin as though you were unequipped to flee from it. Write below three excuses you have made to justify sin in your life.

Remember, His divine power has given you everything you need for life and godliness. You have been set free from the powers of sin and death, so don't willingly walk back into the prison cell of sin and put your shackles back on. Run out and proclaim freedom for other captives instead.

day 8

UM, GUYS?

discover |

> Ask God for boldness to speak up about the gospel. Thank
> Him for awakening you from your sleep before you faced
> the eternal consequences of your sin. Ask Him to help
> you speak up when the time comes. Pray that the Spirit
> would begin working on your friends' hearts right this
> very moment.

READ 1 THESSALONIANS 5:5-10.

For you are all children of light and children of the day. We do not belong to the
night or the darkness. So then, let us not sleep, like the rest, but let us stay awake
and be self-controlled. –1 Thessalonians 5:5-6

"Um, guys?" is the universal thing people say when they are the
first among their friends to see something important approaching.
Whether it is a celebrity or a meteorite heading straight for
Earth, the first person in the group to spot what is significant or
dangerous speaks up to alert the rest. Certainly, we are more
comfortable before we are warned about danger, but would any of
your friends rather not know? Could you see danger approaching
and say nothing?

Even if all of your friends who do not yet know Jesus are running
full-speed into sin, you have the Holy Spirit and are called to self-
control. Paul wrote in verse 8, "But since we belong to the day, let
us be self-controlled and put on the armor of faith and love, and
a helmet of the hope of salvation." You cannot go back to sleep

---

spiritually. Even if you long to join in the sinful activities of what others are doing, you are still called to be a child of light, and this text reminds us that God will not lower the bar.

delight |

Why is day and night a fitting metaphor for contrast between Christians and secular culture?

What does it mean to "belong" to the night, as Paul wrote in verse 5?

What are the commonalities between self-control and Paul's analogy of staying awake?

display |

You cannot go back to sleep spiritually. You cannot un-know the truth about sin and temptation and the spiritual significance of self-control.

List five new goals to go after in your pursuit of self control. Focus your heart on the Spirit and identify ways you have lacked self-control in the past. Remember that these are not a list of "do-nots," but a list of goals. Instead of slamming yourself for failing, aspire to holiness in new ways as a child of the light.

SIN FOR SENSIBILITY

discover |

READ TITUS 2:11-12.

For the grace of God has appeared, bringing salvation for all people, instructing us to deny godlessness and worldly lusts and to live in a sensible, righteous, and godly way in the present age.

Grace changes everything. Grace, by its very nature, is loving treatment that is not deserved. If you deserved it, it would not be grace (Rom. 11:6). If you were so righteous on your own that God had no choice but to treat you fairly and give you heaven, then there would be no grace involved. It would just be a fair transaction of moral virtue. In reality, you were born depraved and sinful, but Christ died for you even while you were still a sinner (Rom. 5:8). What you deserved for your sin was hell, but what you got was grace.

So, how should you respond to this grace? Repenting from sin is the obvious response. Since you have accpted this gift of His grace, it is beyond fair for God to instruct you to deny godlessness and worldly lusts (v.12). Even if your friends who do not yet know Jesus continue in sin, you are called to be holy and to live a sensible, righteous, godly life (v.12). It is the least you could do in light of the tidal wave of grace He lavished upon you.

delight |

Is it possible for someone to proclaim Christ, but not repent of sin? Why or why not?

While the sacrifice of Christ was sufficient to bring salvation for all people (v.11), how does verse 12 distinguish those who are saved from those who are not?

display |

As you grow in Christ, you will begin to understand symptoms of belief versus unbelief. Do not look down on your friends who do not yet know Christ, but see the reflection of your former self in them. Were it not for the appearance of God's grace, you would be doing exactly the same things. Instead, you know true sensibility (v.12). Instead, you are learning self-control.

Look back to your list of goals from the previous devotion. Below, write five ways in which you have traded sin for sensibility.

Pray as Jesus instructed you (Matt. 6:9-13) and ask the Father to deliver you from evil. If you have been losing in the ring of worldly lusts, ask Him to deliver you from temptation. Then walk out of the arena and board the door shut; cutting off the ways you have let temptation into your life. Grace has appeared, so commit once more to live in a godly way (v.12).

day 10

BREAK-IN THE DANCE FLOOR

discover |

> Thank Jesus for the way He defied the crowd with His teaching and even with His silence before angry mobs of mockers. Commit to Him your own willingness to defy the crowd. Pray that nothing short of His perfect will would be done in these difficult days on earth.

READ 2 TIMOTHY 3:1-5.

But know this: Hard times will come in the last days. For people will be lovers of self, lovers of money, boastful, proud, demeaning, disobedient to parents, ungrateful, unholy, unloving, irreconcilable, slanderers, without self-control, brutal, without love for what is good, traitors, reckless, conceited, lovers of pleasure rather than lovers of God, holding to the form of godliness but denying its power. Avoid these people.

Do you have friends who are not afraid to put themselves out there and do something others might think is crazy? If you cannot think of such a friend, then you are likely that friend. The world needs brave souls willing to step out first. Were it not for the first person on the dance floor, everyone would all just stand awkwardly on the side while the music played. In your life, the music is already on, and your faith in Christ already makes you stand out from the crowd, so you might as well dance even if no one else does!

The "last days" (v.1) are the days of human history between the first and the second coming of Christ. You are in the last days now, and this passage tells you clearly to expect them to be hard. Did you notice the words "without self-control" in verse 3? These words were written almost 2,000 years ago, but they sound like a blog post written about culture today. Practicing self-control will, by necessity, cause you to miss out on some pleasure (v. 4), but it is okay because your party will truly begin in heaven—and that party will never end.

delight |

What are some ways you have seen the behaviors listed in verses 2-4 lived out around you?

What does it look like for someone to hold on to a form of godliness, but deny His power in their lives (v. 5)?

display |

Expect to stand out from the crowd because of the gospel. Instead of blending in with a world that does not have your best interests at heart, own the fact that you will stand out. Look back on these years with gratitude that you seized the opportunity rather than with regret that you didn't get on the dance floor.

To be the first on the dance floor takes courage. List four ways you can courageously step out in faith and lead in a way that is opposite of the descriptions listed in 2 Timothy 3:1-5.

How the Holy Spirit Helps When We're Tempted

Throughout Scripture, we see the many roles of the Holy Spirit:

- He helps, reminds and instructs (John 14:26).
- He intercedes for us when we don't know what to pray (Rom. 8:26).
- He produces godly character in our lives (Gal. 5:22-23).
- His presence in our lives marks us as part of God's kingdom (1 Cor. 6:19).
- He is the Helper, the Spirit of truth, and dwells within us (John 14:15-17).
- He brings wisdom and understanding, wise counsel, strength, knowledge and fear of the Lord (Isa. 11:2).
- He empowers us to share the gospel (Acts 1:8).
- He guides us in truth and speaks about the things that will come (John 16:12-15).
- He brings freedom to God's children (2 Cor. 3:17).
- He empowers us to hope, no matter what (Rom. 15:13).
- He convicts of sin (John 16:7-8).
- He helps us to live in obedience to God (Ezek. 36:26-27).
- He teaches us spiritual truths (1 Cor. 2:13).
- He seals us for eternity (Eph. 1:13).

The Holy Spirit marks us as God's own and empowers us to live life His way. We absolutely cannot overcome temptation without Him. This is one of the reasons Scripture calls Him the Helper: He helps us to understand God's Word and obey it. Part of obeying is avoiding sin. Now, this doesn't mean we will live perfectly for the rest of our lives, but that by listening to the Spirit's guidance, we can learn to say no to the things that tempt us.

While the temptations you experience may be different from the temptations your best friend struggles to overcome, "there is nothing new under the sun" (Eccl. 1:9). In other words, there are simply new ways to do the old sins. For example, if you struggle with wanting more followers on social media or obsess over gaining popularity as an influencer, the underlying struggle may be greed, selfishness, insecurity, or arrogance. There are biblical examples of people struggling with this, too. Think about how Martha wanted to be recognized for how hard she worked and served (Luke 10). While it wasn't sinful for her to work hard and serve, her attitude revealed a selfish desire to be noticed.

The Bible gives us timeless wisdom—its commands neither age nor become irrelevant. We can learn, even from narrative stories like that of Martha, how to grow in our relationship with Jesus. But the key thing we need to realize is that, just like Martha, we can't serve God and love others well on our own—we need the Holy Spirit.

Scripture proclaims that "No temptation has come upon you except what is common to humanity. But God is faithful; he will not allow you to be tempted beyond what you are able, but with the temptation he will also provide the way out so that you may be able to bear it" (1 Cor. 10:13). Much like the verse in Ecclesiastes, this verse points out that temptation isn't a new thing. Our being tempted never surprises God—and as He is the God of the universe, it also shouldn't surprise us that He had a plan from the beginning, even for this. But we have to be careful in reading this verse not to think that it says we won't experience temptation. In fact, it declares the opposite: We absolutely will be tempted. However, God will "provide the way out" so that we can withstand the temptation. It's also important to recognize that "what we are able" means "what we can withstand with the power of the Holy Spirit." We can't do this on our own; it is the Holy Spirit who empowers us to live out the Christian life and escape temptation.

Through the power of the Holy Spirit, we can face whatever comes our way with "love, joy, peace, patience, kindness, goodness, faithfulness, gentleness, and self-control" (Gal. 5:22-23). But this is something, just like following Jesus, that we have to choose. We have to choose to set aside our desires in favor of God's each day. We cannot be self-controlled unless we are Spirit-controlled. As we embrace the Christian life and the role of the Holy Spirit in our lives, we can learn to say no to what tempts us and fully embrace the beauty of following God wherever He leads and whatever He leads us to do.

day 11

SLAM THE GATES

discover

> Invite the Holy Spirit to examine your heart for areas where you've been weak. Recognize that as He does, it will likely illuminate something difficult to give up. Remember that holiness is worth any sacrifice. Recognize also that these convictions are unique to you and that others who do not follow Christ are not held to them. Ask Him to guard your heart and speech from looking and speaking down to others who do not do the same.

READ 1 PETER 5:8.

Be sober-minded, be alert. Your adversary the devil is prowling around like a roaring lion, looking for anyone he can devour.

Do you know those sweet Bible verses that people make into sepia-toned memes with soft cursive writing over a picture of steam rising from a coffee cup that is sitting on a wooden table on a deck overlooking a peaceful lake? Today's text is not one of those. The thought of being hunted by a lion like Mowgli in The Jungle Book is unsettling. Passages like today's text are not popular, but they are in the Word of God for a reason. You need to know this. God desires to warn us of the dangers of our enemy.

Verses like this are incredibly important. If we only had the uplifting verses, we would be unprepared for the reality that is in front of us as followers of Christ. Therefore, we must take to heart Peter's instruction to be sober-minded. Another way to put it is that we must be totally aware of the devil's goals and plans. He wants to devour you. Therefore, we should slam the gates on him and cling tightly to self-control from the Holy Spirit.

delight |

What does the word "prowling" indicate about Satan's approach?

What evidence have you seen of the enemy in your life recently?

display |

One of the deepest lies that Satan convinces people of is that he is not real and that God is to blame for the terrible things that happen everyday. Yes, God is in ultimate control, but Satan is responsible for every bad thing that has ever happened. His time of reckoning has been prophesied and set, but it's not yet here. Until then, we must remain ever-vigilant, sober-minded, and alert to the powers of evil at work in our world. Be aware today of his active prowling, watch for the paw prints, and lock the gates that might be ajar in your life.

Lock out the lion. Slam shut any gates of technology, movies, music, and conversations through which this prowling and roaring lion has devoured your purity in the recent past. Be drastic if necessary. Cut out of your life anything that has caused you personally to stumble (Matt. 5:27-30). List three ways you can slam the gate on the devil's plans to devour you today.

SUBMISSION

discover

Therefore, submit to God. Resist the devil, and he will flee from you. -James 4:7

In a wrestling match, the goal is to either pin your opponent's shouluders to the mat or to get them to submit. To submit means to give up. The word submission often carries a negative connotation. It implies that you gave up unwillingly. But when you submit to God, you are not really giving up; you are giving yourself over to Him. Being in His hands is the only place you will ever find complete protection.

When you submit to God, He towers over you, and the evil one pursuing you has to flee. Verse 6 quotes Proverbs 3:34, revealing that God gives grace to the humble. It requires humility to submit to God, but the benefit of having the enemy flee from you is totally worth it.

Refusal to resist the devil is basically submission to him, and you cannot submit to both God and the devil. So, choose. Look closely at the final words in verse 7. God is omnipresent; the devil is not. God goes with you wherever you are, but the devil does not. The devil is given a degree of freedom for now (Rev. 20:7-10), but even then, he can only tempt you to the extent that God allows him to (Job 1:6-12). The Bible promises that Satan will flee if you resist him.

> Put your submission to God into words and speak those words to Him. Ask Him for increased vigilance so that you can sense and resist the enemy's attacks.

delight |

When you resist the attacks of Satan, who is he actually fleeing from?

Reflect on a time when you submitted to God and resisted the devil. How did you do it and how did it make you feel?

display |

In the chart below, list benefits of submitting to God and the cost of not resisting the devil. Remember, submission to God is nothing to be ashamed of. You are submitting to your Savior, who loves you dearly and gave Himself for you. You are running from death and gaining life.

Benefits of Submission to God   Cost of not resisting the devil

day 13

DON'T THINK ABOUT PIZZA

discover |

Ask the Holy Spirit to bring Scripture to your mind and
show you how to apply it in steps throughout the day.
Thank God for being our Immanuel; our God who is with
us. Thank Him for being the Wonderful Counselor who
never leaves us. This is your first step today.

READ GALATIANS 5:16.

*I say, then, walk by the Spirit and you will certainly not carry out the desire of
the flesh.*

Whatever you do right now, do not think about pizza. Absolutely
do not imagine the strings the cheese makes when you lift a hot
slice out of the box. Do not think about a steamy garlic parmesan
crust, or the buttery crunch it makes when you bite into it.
Whatever you do, do not think about the savory toppings. Now,
what are you thinking about? Pizza, of course. That is how it goes
when you think constantly about not sinning.

Walking by the Spirit is about more than just abstaining from sin:
it is about doing God's will. Living a holy lifestyle is not a negative
action; like simply refusing to do something. It's a positive and
deliberate series of actions toward God, taken in obedience by the
Spirit's prompting. We walk one step at a time. When you focus
only on the next step the Spirit has for you, there is no room for the
desire of the flesh. So, Paul using the word "certainly" in this verse
is not an overstatement. Do you see? When you focus entirely on
one thing you forget the other. For example, you have already
forgotten about pizza...until now.

delight |

Even though you are a believer, why are you still vulnerable to temptation from Satan?

Why do you think this verse uses the word "walk" by the Spirit instead of "sit" by the Spirit?

display |

If you have been focusing on what not to do, it is time to turn your view of self-control upside down. Realign your focus, and the rest will follow. If you focus on your temptation, it will constantly be on your mind. If you focus on the Spirit of God and what you are learning from God's Word, self-control will come more easily. The Spirit's voice will become more easy to recognize. The Holy Spirit will speak through His Word and show you the next step of obedience.

Listen today as the Spirit reminds you of Scripture. Each time you are reminded of a verse from the Bible, write it down or leave a voice note on your phone. At the end of the day, review all those remembrances. Then, celebrate His work in your life...over pizza.

day 14

RULE OVER IT

discover |

READ GENESIS 4:3-8.

Then the Lord said to Cain, "Why are you furious? And why do you look despondent? If you do what is right, won't you be accepted? But if you do not do what is right, sin is crouching at the door. Its desire is for you, but you must rule over it." Cain said to his brother Abel, "Let's go out to the field." And while they were in the field, Cain attacked his brother Abel and killed him. –Genesis 4:6-8

Scripture does not record exactly what God expected from Cain and Able's sacrifices, but Cain knew the expectation (v.7) and did not bring it. Abel was keeper of the flocks and Cain worked in the fields. Abel brought the biggest and fattest offering he could, while Cain's offering of produce from the fields was not what was required. On top of that, his offering was given while evil was in his heart (1 John 3:12). God accepted Abel's offering, but not Cain's. This led to resentment, which led to sin, and ultimately culminated in Cain committing the first murder.

The truth is: the whole point of sin is our destruction. Satan wants to rule over us and he does that through sin. If we are casual about sin—as Cain was about his offering—then it will master us. As it masters us, our lives will spiral out of control.

Thankfully, Jesus gave Himself as the ultimate sacrafice for our sin. As you continually walk with Him in trust and obedience, He will help you master sin, which will lead to life.

delight |

Which words from verse 8 show that Cain planned ahead to murder his brother?

Do you ever do something knowing that it will probably lead you to sin? What steps can you take to deliberately walk away from sin?

display |

The day is prophesied and approaching where Satan will be forever destroyed, but you are reading this because that day has not yet come. Until then, sin still crouches at the door, and you, like Cain, are still called to rule over it (v.7). You are called to self-control. 1 Corinthians 10:13 gives you great hope, though. God will not allow you to be tempted beyond what you can bear.

One of the best ways to rule over sin is to have active accountability in your life. Find someone of the same gender who will hold you accountable. This person needs to be someone you will be honest with, because you will be tempted to lie to him/her. If you already have an accountability partner in your life, get in touch with him/her and let them know that you appreciate the role they are playing in your life to help you rule over sin.

Share with God your respect for His warning to Cain that sin crouches at the door. Ask Him to help you rule over sin. Ask Him to lead you away from temptation. Pray for self-control.

IN CONTEXT

discover |

READ MATTHEW 4:1-11.

Again, the devil took him to a very high mountain and showed him all the kingdoms of the world and their splendor. And he said to him, "I will give you all these things if you will fall down and worship me." Then Jesus told him, "Go away, Satan! For it is written: Worship the Lord your God, and serve only him." Then the devil left him, and angels came and began to serve him.
–Matthew 4:8-11

Remember the scene in *The Lion King* where Mufasa brings Simba to the top of the mountain and shows him the entire kingdom? He told him that everything the light touched belonged to them. Satan did the same thing to Jesus in these verses today. One thing he failed to remember is that you can't give away what you don't own.

This passage is often taught to show how Jesus used Scripture to fight temptation. What is often omitted in that teaching is the fact that Satan actually quoted the Bible to tempt Jesus. The critical difference between the way Satan used the Bible and Jesus used the Bible is that Jesus used Scripture in context. In fact, if Satan had kept reading the Scripture he quoted to try to tempt Jesus (Ps. 91:11), he would have gotten to verse 13, which explains that the Messiah would trample the serpent. It's important to know the context of a passage before you quote it.

> Ask God for spiritual protection. Ask Him to rebuke Satan and to deliver you from evil, casting away forces of spiritual darkness from you and your family today.

delight |

How did Jesus practice the instruction of James 4:7 in the Scripture for today?

Satan's original sins were pride and the desire to be like the Most High. Where is that motive present in this text?

display |

When you focus on a passage of Scripture, read the whole passage. To interpret the Bible properly, you need to know context. Jesus, being the Word in flesh Himself (John 1:1), knew where the Bible verses He used fit in the larger picture of redemption and was able to use Scripture properly as a weapon against the enemy. The devil, meanwhile, deliberately removed context from the verses he used in a futile attempt to attack the Word Himself with the Word.

The reason Satan couldn't give Jesus all the Kingdoms of the world was because he didn't own them (Psalm 24:1). Satan doesn't own you—God does. On an index card, write the words "I am His." Keep it in your pocket, purse, or nearby so that you will be constantly reminded of this truth all day.

I have treasured your word in my heart so that I may not sin against you.

PSALM 119:11

day 16

THE WAY OUT

discover|

READ 1 CORINTHIANS 10:13.

No temptation has come upon you except what is common to humanity. But God is faithful; he will not allow you to be tempted beyond what you are able, but with the temptation he will also provide the way out so that you may be able to bear it.

Imagine you are trapped in a maze. Everything looks the same; there are no distinguishing marks no matter where you go. With every turn, you get more and more panicked. Then, you make a turn, and you see a faint glimmer of light. As you get closer to the light, you can clearly see how to escape the maze. At that point, would you turn around and look for another way to get out, or would you take the path before you?

As long as you are alive, you will face temptation from time to time; but know that God loves you. As revealed in 1 Corinthians 10:13, He will always provide a way out from temptation. Our job is to take the way out that He provides.

When Satan tempted Job, God gave Satan parameters that he had to abide by while attacking Job. He does the same on your behalf. The words "except what is common to humanity" shows that you aren't tempted in any unique way from anyone else. These are God's words, and He promised to always give you a way out of temptation. It is up to you to rely on the Holy Spirit and practice self-control to follow the light to the exit each time.

delight |

How have you experienced God's faithfulness when you've been tempted?

Why is it important to understand that all people face the same kinds of temptations?

display |

It's often hard to turn down temptation. However, when you are weak, God is mighty (2 Cor. 12:9-10). He never puts you in any situation that He cannot handle. He provides the way out, and He bears the weight so that you can handle the strain of it. You just have to delcare your dependence on Him and follow as He leads you out.

Look around your house and find a flashlight. Throw it in your book bag or purse. Everytime you see it, click it on and off. Let it serve as a reminder that God's word is a light to your feet (Psalm 119:105). His Word will help you find the way out from temptation.

Proclaim to God your belief in this verse and declare your dependance on Him. Express your appreciation for the escape plan He offers and commit to Him that you will seek to take the way out that He provides.

day 17

WEAKNESS > STRENGTH

discover |

Humbly stand before God and admit that you are weak. Then, ask Him to take your weaknesses and, through His strength, turn them around and use them for His glory.

READ 2 CORINTHIANS 12:6-10.

But he said to me, "My grace is sufficient for you, for my power is perfected in weakness." Therefore, I will most gladly boast all the more about my weaknesses, so that Christ's power may reside in me. -2 Corinthians 12:9

In a famous Old Testament battle, God whittled down the size of Israel's army from 22,000 to 300. He took away their traditional weapons and told them to blow horns, shatter pitchers, and raise torches (Judg. 7). He did this so that Israel would not "elevate themselves over me and say, 'I saved myself'" (Judg. 7:2b). He actually made the army weaker so that His strength would shine through and save the day.

God specializes in using the weak to accomplish things beyond their strength. In doing so, He brings glory to Himself instead of to the earthly vessel through whom He worked (2 Cor. 4:7). The apostle Paul knew this all too well. He was given what he called a "thorn in the flesh" (v.7) so that he would continually rely on God's grace and strength. This wasn't God making it hard on Paul; it was God's way of showing Paul how much He could do through him if he was reliant on God's strength rather than his own. The same is true for you.

delight |

What was Paul's response to the "torment" he experienced?

How have you seen God's power perfected in your weakness?

display |

These verses make it clear that even a person with extraordinary willpower is weak in comparison to God. When He makes us painfully aware of our weakness, it's just an opportunity to rely more on His strength.

Make a list below of three weaknesses you have. Beside each one, write a way God can bring Himself glory and reveal His extraordinary strength through your weaknesses.

day 18

VITAMINS TO TREASURE

discover|

> Talk to God about your appreciation for His Word. Confess if you have not treasured it as you should. Ask God for new ways to take in more of His Word and become better equipped to face temptation through it.

READ PSALM 119:11.

I have treasured your word in my heart so that I may not sin against you.

Gummy vitamins are good for you and are surprisingly delicious. However, they are not enough to sustain life. In addition to vitamins, you need food, water, sleep, etc., or you will die. These devotions are like vitamins. Through them you can focus hard on just a few verses at a time and apply them. But spending a few minutes a day in this book is not enough to keep you alive spiritually. You must couple this time with prayer, worship, and being taught the truths of God's Word.

Jesus, as the embodiment of the Word Himself (John 1:1), knew how to perfectly use Scripture to combat temptation. As you grow in your devotional life and learn more Scripture, you are better equipped to fight temptation and grow in self-control. So, in all the ways you take in Scripture, make sure it seeps into your heart. Treasure it to your core, and the Spirit will remind you of it when temptation arises. Look at the direct connection between treasuring God's Word and victory over sin in this verse. If you want to fight against sin, you need to treasure Scripture.

delight |

What is something you treasure? How do you make it clear that you treasure this item?

What is the difference between empty memorization of Scripture and treasuring God's Word in your heart?

display |

If you do not already, add to your Bible intake regimen a supplement beyond the few verses we cover at a time in this devotion. Be sure that your study of Scripture is not simply to increase your academic knowledge of the Bible. Instead, in honor of today's verse, view Scripture as a treasure. It is the ultimate source of truth, so hiding more of it in your very core equips you with a greater arsenal to fight temptation and grow in self-control.

With permission, listen to the Bible on audio through an app or device while traveling to and from school or other activities. Consider the Gospel of John as an excellent starting point. The Gospel of John was originally written to convince Gentiles that Jesus is God, and it still has that effect today! So, as you grow in self-control, you will also be better equipped for evangelism—sharing your faith with others.

day 19

WHAT'S INSIDE

---

discover

READ 2 TIMOTHY 1:7.

For God has not given us a spirit of fear, but one of power, love, and sound judgment.

Have you ever had to navigate your house with the lights off? As long as there are no unexpected obstacles on the floor—your little sister's toys, your big brother's size 13 tennis shoes, or piles of folded towels your parents haven't put up yet— you can probably do it fairly easily. Why? Because you know what you have inside your house. Today's Scripture reminds you of what you have from God. Rather than a spirit of fear, God has given you power, love, and sound judgment.

Instead of being fearful of what's around the corner, you have the power to trust God's goodness. Instead of being afraid of being alone, you know that His love will never leave you or forsake you. Instead of being overwhelmed with heart palpitations at the mere thought of temptation, you remember that God's Spirit has given you sound judgment to resist. Remember the source of what's inside you is from Him. Therefore, you can navigate life—even the unexpected obstacles—with His power, love, and sound judgment.

> Pray this verse today. Trade your fear for His power. Trade your fear for love because God's perfect love casts out all fear (1 John 4:18). Trade your fear of rejection for trust that the judgment God gives you is sound.

delight |

Because God has not given us a spirit of fear, where does fear come from?

How does this verse speak into self-control and avoiding temptation?

display |

This verse was originally written by the apostle Paul to a young pastor named Timothy. You can probably easily put yourselves in Timothy's shoes because you are young and have likely faced challenging circumstances where you had to choose God's power, love, and sound judgment over fear.

List two scenarios below where you might lean toward fear. Then reflect on the truth of this verse and write out how God's power, love, and sound judgment might help you overcome that fear.

day 20

WEAK SPOTS

discover |

> Talk to God with complete honesty about what you desire.
> Be forthright about the things you want to do that honor
> Him and about the evil desires that still live within you that
> you need Him to help you overcome.

*No one undergoing a trial should say, "I am being tempted by God," since God
is not tempted by evil, and he himself doesn't tempt anyone. But each person is
tempted when he is drawn away and enticed by his own evil desire.
–James 1:13–14*

It's 12:30 p.m. on a Tuesday. Your stomach is churning from the
sloppy joe you just wolfed down in the school cafeteria, and
you're incredibly nervous about the test the teacher is handing
out right now. As you begin taking the test, you find it to be more
challenging than you thought it would be. Suddenly, you remember
the girl next to you is the smartest person in the class. If you tilt
your head juuuust right you can see directly onto her page. Here's
the question: is your desire to cheat the teacher's fault?

Of course not! This scenario also explains the Scripture for today.
Yes, there are times in life when God allows your faith to be tested,
but God never tempts you to sin. You are tempted by the sin
nature that you were born with, combined with your own desires.
Therefore, you have to know your weak spots. You have to be
aware of situations that might tempt you and rely on His Spirit
to show you the way out when temptation is unavoidable (see
Day 16).

LifeWay Students | Devotions   50

delight |

Who is exempt from temptation? Which words in James 1:13-14 give you the answer?

This verse uses the words "drawn away." What and who are we being drawn away from by temptation?

display |

Recognize what is happening when temptation strikes. See the bait on the hook for what it is. Know yourself and your weak spots. The truth is that everyone is born with natural desire toward sin. You will be waging war with this natural inclination until you get to heaven. You are an eternal soul inside an imperfect body, housing the perfect Holy Spirit. When you achieve victory over temptation through the Spirit, you take a step forward in your pursuit of holiness.

On Day 14, you were encouraged to find an accountability partner. If you have not already, establish accountability with someone of your same gender in your life who is also growing in Christ. Check in with your accountability partner today and see how you can pray for him/her. If you don't have one yet, pray that God would connect you with someone you can share your life with and walk together in faithfulness to God.

Respond vs. React

The truth of the matter is that people will do and say things that irritate, hurt, or upset us. But we can choose what we will do when this inevitably happens: We can choose to react or respond. Here's a simple way to distinguish between reacting and responding: a reaction is an impulse, gut-level action or reply, while a response is made after taking time to think through what has been said and giving a careful reply.

Scripture cautions us to be slow to respond to hurtful words and actions: "Everyone should be quick to listen, slow to speak, and slow to anger" (Jas. 1:19). How can we do this right in the middle of a difficult situation? Let's take a look at a three-step process to help us.

Be quick to listen. Learn to listen for what someone says and what he or she doesn't say. Watch body language and facial expressions, and listen to tone of voice. For example, crossed arms could indicate defensiveness, or tapping fingers could mean impatience. Eye contact and standing up straight usually point to confidence, while smiling to the point where your eyes crinkle makes people appear warm and welcoming.[2] The volume, speed, and even breathiness with which we speak also communicates something about our underlying feelings.

If we're quick to listen, we'll take a step back and look at the bigger picture. We'll wonder what's going on in that person's life in this moment and outside of it. As you're paying attention to tone, body language, and facial cues, it is still important to listen to the words someone says. Do they repeat words or is there a common theme? Listen attentively.

Then, take a deep breath before you respond. For one, this calms you and helps you to think clearer. Breathing deeply also creates space to remember that God cares about the pain you're feeling in that moment and the pain the one who hurt you may be feeling as well. So, give your cares over to Him (1 Pet. 5:7).

Be slow to speak. This means letting what you've heard sink in before you respond. Before you try to figure out how what someone said relates to you, continue on with your listening skills to make sure you've understood. Here, it can be a good idea to summarize aloud for someone what you understood him or her to say. Then, check for understanding with a statement like, "I want to make sure I understand. Is this what you meant?" Give your friend a chance to respond, then summarize and clarify again before moving forward. This ensures that you truly understand what it is you're responding to, and that allows the other person to feel like you value his or her thoughts, feelings, and words.

Now, take a beat to ask yourself if what your friend is saying is accurate. If it is, apologize. Then, ask God to help you change your response in the future. It can also be helpful to ask something like: "How can I word things differently in the future? I want to speak the truth in a way that's helpful to you rather than harmful." If not, think about this person. What's his or her character like? What's going on in his or her life? How might that be causing him or her to speak to you? Then, consider saying something like, "It sounds like you're having a rough morning. What can I do to help?" Sometimes, all others need to know is that someone cares and is there to listen and help.

Be slow to anger. You'll notice that all three of these actions—even if they are an active waiting—connect and build on one another. Part of being slow to anger is continuing to consider the bigger picture. But here, we want to focus on the biggest picture. Rather than only looking at what's going on in that person's life, we want to look to what God says to do. We look to His character and His plan to guide our responses. Here are three key things to remember:

- Every person, regardless of how he or she treats you, is made in the image of God.
- God has the ultimate say: He is the one who gets to decide when and what consequences people will receive when they treat others poorly.
- God calls us to love others as He has loved us—basically, we love no matter what (John 13:34; 1 John 4:19).

If someone is unkind or hurtful to you out of spite, you are still called to respond in love and kindness. Now, this doesn't mean being a doormat. You can kindly set boundaries for how you will or won't be treated and clearly communicate those. This is a loving action both for yourself and others. However, at the end of the day you belong to God, and everything you say and do reflects on Him. When someone hurts you and you haven't sinned against him or her (or have apologized for sinning against him or her), then remember that the situation rests securely in God's hands. What better place could it be? Ultimately, God is the one who will set all things right (Rom. 12:19).

My Story

Take a minute to write about a difficult situation you're experiencing. In a journal, write out how you can engage with that person by using the three-step process outlined in James 1:19. Then pray that God would give you the strength and wisdom to carry it out.

day 21

MEASURE TWICE, CUT ONCE

discover |

> Ask God to prepare your heart to receive a difficult truth from His Word today. Ask for His help in seeing yourself accurately. Commit to listen to what the Spirit is about to tell you about your anger, speech, and ability to listen.

READ JAMES 1:19-21.

My dear brothers and sisters, understand this: Everyone should be quick to listen, slow to speak, and slow to anger, for human anger does not accomplish God's righteousness. -James 1:19-20

In carpentry, there is a saying that goes, "Measure twice, cut once." What it means is that once you cut on a board, you can't put it back together. So, take careful measurements, making sure it's exactly what you need, then confidently make your cut, knowing that it's accurate. This is the perfect illustration of what James was explaining in the Scripture for today.

Notice the order he gave in verse 19. It all starts with listening well. Speaking too quickly indicates that you probably have not listened well because it is physically impossible to speak and give your full listening attention to someone else at the same time. If you listen well and measure your words carefully, you are less inclined to melt down into anger. When you get to the point that you are fuming mad, you've ceased to be able to accomplish God's righteousness in that moment. Therefore, you need to measure your words twice and cut once with what you say so that you don't descend into an angry rage and momentarily lose all effectiveness for the gospel and God's glory.

delight |

Why is human anger incompatible with God's righteousness?

List three people who are "quick to listen" and describe how you feel about each of them.

display | .

One of the keys to being quick to listen, slow to speak, and slow to anger is to have a teachable spirit. If you feel like you know it all or are always right, you'll be less inclined to listen. You'll feel like you have the answer and everyone should listen to what you have to say. Then if they don't listen to you, you'll get angry. See how the cycle works?

Measure twice and cut once today. Try to strike corrective phrases like, "Actually..." and "But listen to me..." from your vocabulary for one day. Keep a tally of how many times you refrain from inserting your opinion based on thinking you are correct about something.

However, if there are moments when you do need to assert a correct understanding about someone or something (especially if it's a spiritual matter), still measure twice and cut once. Season your words with grace (Col. 4:6) so that you might be heard rather than dismissed as a know-it-all.

day 22

THE WRONG QUESTION

discover |

READ 1 THESSALONIANS 4:3-8.

It is God's will that you should be sanctified: that you should avoid sexual immorality; that each of you should learn to control your own body in a way that is holy and honorable, not in passionate lust like the Gentiles, who do not know God. -1 Thessalonians 4:3-5

The classic question every teenager asks when it comes to dating—"How far is too far?"— is the wrong question. The desired answer is a clear line where everything less is okay and everything beyond is not. Here's the bottom line: There is a time and a place for physical intimacy and that place is marriage. Yes, the standard is high, but we are called to the highest standard of holiness.

To be sanctified is to be set apart. This is one aspect of God's will for your life and future that you can know with absolute certainty because of verse 4. This applies to every part of your existence. Is your online activity holy and honorable? Is every physical interaction with your boyfriend or girlfriend holy and honorable? Those who worshiped false gods in Paul's day did not have the convicting presence of the Holy Spirit that you have. So, control your own body and make drastic sacrifices to avoid sexual immorality; not sneak closer to it.

delight |

How does avoiding sexual immorality lead to sanctification?

It is your responsibility to learn to control your own body, but you are not alone in this pursuit. How does God help you learn to do this?

display |

The reason the classic question is the wrong question is because it looks in the wrong direction, asking, "How close can I get to sin?" The better question and proper view is to ask, "How close can I get to holiness?" If a given action leads toward sexual immorality rather than away from it, eliminate it. Self-control is a matter of holiness. So, draw toward holiness rather than away from it.

Sacrifice devices that cause you to stumble. Slaughter your access to pornography on the altar of holiness. If you cannot function scholastically or professionally without devices, then work with your family to lock your devices down with accountability software and, even then, establish an open and brutally honest accountability relationship with someone you trust.

Ready your heart to proclaim to God that holiness matters more to you than momentary pleasure that takes you a step away from His will for you. Always remember to abide in His grace for you when you fall.

MOST OF THE MINUTES

discover |

> Speak with God about where you stand regarding alcohol before you are of the legal age to drink. Resolve now to show self-control in this regard. If you have stumbled with drugs or alcohol, confess it before God and rest in the grace He pours on you.

READ EPHESIANS 5:15-21.

Pay careful attention, then, to how you walk—not as unwise people but as wise— making the most of the time, because the days are evil. So don't be foolish, but understand what the Lord's will is. And don't get drunk with wine, which leads to reckless living, but be filled by the Spirit. -Ephesians 5:15-18

The final minutes of a close sporting event are often quite exciting. Whether a team is trying to score a last minute touchdown or prevent its opponent from making a game winning basket, the final moments are vital to the outcome of a game. For this reason, when a player is disengaged or not giving everything he or she has as the seconds melt away, fans often react ... let's call it ... passionately.

The Scripture for today explored this same idea, but from a spiritual perspective. Unlike sports, you do not know how much time is left on your life's clock. Hopefully you'll have more decades to come, but you cannot know that for sure. The apostle Paul encouraged the Ephesians to acknowledge this uncertainty and embrace their time on earth by making the most of it. As a result of the presence of the Holy Spirit in your life and the unknown number of days you have left, you should do the same. This means it is unwise to waste your days abusing substances like drugs and alcohol.

delight |

How does abusing drugs and alcohol lead to reckless living?

How does choosing to be filled with the Holy Spirit help you avoid the recklessness brought on by substance abuse?

display |

Prepare to be conspicuous. You have a higher calling on your life than drunkenness and drugs can give you. Just as you do with sexual purity, control your body in a way that is holy and honorable. Imagine the trajectory that drugs and drunkenness set for your future, then imagine yourself giving an account before God for the time spent giving in to the evil desires that decreased your abilities to honor Him in those thousands of wasted minutes.

Write out a quick rundown of your daily schedule below. Pray over it and ask God to help you make the most of the day. If you are tempted to abuse drugs or alcohol, think about how that would cost you the productivity of the day, both personally and for the Kingdom of God.

SPEAKING LIFE

discover |

READ EPHESIANS 4:25-31.

Therefore, putting away lying, speak the truth, each one to his neighbor, because we are members of one another. Be angry and do not sin. Don't let the sun go down on your anger, and don't give the devil an opportunity.
–Ephesians 4:25–27

We've seen that self-control is demonstrated in our bodily conduct, but what about the way we talk to people? Through our words we share the message of the gospel, and the Holy Spirit changes people's hearts. Honoring God with our whole selves means exercising self-control in our speech too.

> Confess to God any lingering lies you have told and set the record straight if possible. Pray for the strength to make peace with others where you can. Ask God to deliver your speech from evil and to use your tongue for good.

In three different verses in today's Scripture, Paul laid out areas of speech that the Ephesians needed to bring under the Lordship of Christ. Verse 25 listed lying—intentionally deceiving others with words. In verse 29, Paul mentioned foul language and tearing others down. Finally, in verse 31, he called out shouting and slandering others with words. Each of these things are different, but all are carried out through speech. With your words, you have the opportunity to speak grace into the lives of others; to be a blessing and not a curse. Words can bring hope or destruction; they can even lead to eternal life or death. You just have to decide how you will let the Lord use your words.

delight |

Why is it important to God that members of a church not lie to one another?

What are some opportunity areas in your life the devil may seize to tempt you into sinful speech?

display |

Spirit-filled Christians do not slander people or seek revenge to get back at others with their words. It's confusing for people to hear profanity and songs of praise come from the same lips. Seek to let your words always point to God and His goodness.

Take an inventory of your words and eliminate those that hinder your ability to share the gospel. Then, replace them with encouraging words to others. Trade bitterness for grace and watch as people respond to the positivity, hope, and encouragement you bring to their lives through your words.

day 25

ONLINE LEGACY

discover |

> Even if you do not participate in social media, pray that
> God continues to shape the way you speak to people. Give
> Him your voice and ask Him to take over your words so
> that they give life to others.

READ COLOSSIANS 4:5-6.

*Act wisely toward outsiders, making the most of the time. Let your speech always
be gracious, seasoned with salt, so that you may know how you should answer
each person.*

Imagine it's thirty years in the future. You are sitting around the
dinner table with your family when one of your children—who is
the age you are now— pulls up your Instagram timeline and starts
going backwards. What would they find? What would they think
about the posts they would see from your teenage years? Your
generation will have a written and pictorial legacy that will be
preserved online forever. What is your online legacy? What do your
posts say about your relationship with Chirst?

Food seasoned with salt tastes better, so gracious words on social
media are like delicious food. As verse 5 noted, you must be wise
in your interactions toward those outside the Christian faith; this
includes your online interactions. When your online words are
not gracious, it reflects not just on you, but on your church, your
brothers and sisters in Christ, and on Jesus Himself. Along with
the occasional funny cat video, what better purpose could there
be for your online platform than to help others know and see the
goodness of God on display? Your words on social media must also
be included in your practice of self-control.

delight |

List three ways you can leverage your online presence to glorify God and help others know Christ.

What does it mean in verse six when it says "you may know how you should answer each person"?

display |

In Matthew 28:18-20, Jesus gave us the Great Commission, sending us out to make disciples of all nations. This is why we are called to act wisely toward those who do not yet believe in Jesus. A foolish social media post or reply in a comment thread can shut someone's ears to the gospel. Sharing things that are untrue robs you of credibility. Making your profile into a shrine about how awesome you are worships self instead of God. Blatant use of profanity sends a mixed message when you also proclaim Christ. Instead, let your social media presence be always gracious (v. 6).

People who learn that you stand for the gospel may scour your profile to see if you are the real deal. The good news is that you have the ability, and even the obligation, to remove past posts that no longer line up with your convictions. Delete any past social media posts that don't bring honor to God. With parental permission, share John 3:16 online. Let any discussion you have as a result of the post be seasoned with grace.

My dear brothers and sisters, understand this: Everyone should be quick to listen, slow to speak, and

slow to anger,
for human
anger does not
accomplish God's
righteousness.

JAMES 1:19-20

COVERED IN DUST

discover |

> Right now, ask God to help you see all that you have as His, especially money. Submit your financial resources, great or small, to the Lordship of Christ.

READ MATTHEW 6:19-24.

Don't store up for yourselves treasures on earth, where moth and rust destroy and where thieves break in and steal. But store up for yourselves treasures in heaven, where neither moth nor rust destroys, and where thieves don't break in and steal. For where your treasure is, there your heart will be also. –Matthew 6:19-21

There are things in your attic or garage right now that you once cherished. They are covered in dust. Ebay, Craig's List, and other online platforms are packed with junk for sale by people who once clamored to have these things. People once stood in line for hours to be the first to have phones that are now obsolete. Stuff, no matter how expensive or in demand it might be, is finite. One day, it will all be worthless and go away.

What you do with money and your things indicates what is happening in your heart. Verse 24 says, "No one can serve two masters, since either he will hate one and love the other, or he will be devoted to one and despise the other. You cannot serve both God and money." People can end up worshiping money and things, banking their lives on stuff that does not last forever, while going bankrupt with their souls that will live for eternity. We are all tempted to give a higher priority to money and our physical things, but these things must be mastered in self-control also.

delight |

What is something that you once wanted so badly but now is collecting dust somewhere? What can you learn about this that will guide you in the future?

How do you store up for yourself treasure in heaven?

display |

Check your heart for bad spending habits. If you are prone to chasing the latest fad that will soon go out of style and be discarded, pray honestly about what that says about your heart and its desire for the things of this world.

Think about the last three things you desperately wanted. List them below. Beside those three things, write ways that object can bring glory to God. If it is something that leads you away from God, think about ways that you can reverse that trend. Finally, think about that one thing you desperately want right now. Is it something that will be collecting dust in a matter of time? Is it something that leads you away from God? Consider that maybe you don't need it as desperately as you thought.

day 27

HIS TEMPLE

discover |

Pray that God prepares your heart to hear a tough truth today. Proclaim to God your solid belief in His love for you as His child. Tell Him that He is Lord over every aspect of your life. Then, rooted in His love for you, follow the Holy Spirit where He takes you with this Scripture—even if it is painful at first.

READ PROVERBS 23:19-21.

For the drunkard and the glutton will become poor, and grogginess will clothe them in rags. –Proverbs 23:21

We have to practice self-control in all areas of our lives. We can't pick and choose what we allow God to wrestle under self-control in our lives and what we don't. Today, the Scripture mentioned two areas, one of which many of us struggle to bring under self-control.

These two areas are alcohol (covered in Day 23) and gluttony. Gluttony, or overeating, is something that often gets swept under the rug. There are a variety of reasons why people overeat, ranging from emotions to a simple lack of nutritional understanding. The point is not to shame anyone. However, it is to make it very clear that what and how much we eat matters. This, too, must be an area we practice self-control in.

We must remember that our bodies are a temple of the Lord (1 Cor. 6:19-20). Therefore, we must not misuse our bodies by being gluttonous. If our bodies are unhealthy, we are not as useful to the Lord as we could be. So, we must treat our bodies right, by eating as healthy as we can and exercising.

delight |

Why is it helpful to project where our behaviors ultimately take us?

What effects can chronic overeating have on your future?

display |

Verse 20 says, "Don't associate with those who drink too much wine or with those who gorge themselves on meat." Look around your life. Are you being influenced in unhealthy ways? Is it time to break ranks and set your mind on the right course (v. 20) in defiance of those who have been steering you in the wrong direction with food and alcohol?

Look at your reflection and see a beloved child of God above all else. Then, look honestly and see if there are opportunities to grow in self-control. Look honestly at the straight line that connects your choices to your physical well-being. The great news is that self-control comes from the Holy Spirit. This is a spiritual matter and, as God's beloved child, you are not alone in this. You are His. On day 15, you were challenged to write on an index card, "I am His." Find that card again and underline the phrase written there. If you didn't do it before, do it this time. Keep that card close by all day. Let it serve as a reminder that you are His beloved child, special and wonderful. Let it encourage you toward self-control in all areas of life.

day 28

DON'T RUIN THE BROWNIES

discover |

READ ROMANS 8:7-9.

The mindset of the flesh is hostile to God because it does not submit to God's law. Indeed, it is unable to do so. Those who are in the flesh cannot please God. You, however, are not in the flesh, but in the Spirit, if indeed the Spirit of God lives in you. If anyone does not have the Spirit of Christ, he does not belong to him.

The most delectable batch of brownies ever baked is coming out of your oven right now. Can you smell them? Picture the mysteriously dark, rich, batter, thick with designer chocolate and luxuriously laced with a drizzle of molten caramel on top. Feel the crisp crunch of the roasted pecans...unless you are allergic to them. There is just one thing: the baker added one teaspoon of bird droppings to the batter before she put them in the oven!

Take this idea and apply it to sin. There is no such thing as a little bit of sin. Mixing a little bit of sin in our lives is like mixing a teaspoon of bird droppings into the brownie batter. If you are going to walk with the Holy Spirit, you have to be all in. Do not ruin what He wants to do in your life with "just" a teaspoon of sin that you tolerate. Repentance means turning away from sin. Do not let just a little bit of your former life— which was hostile to God —remain in your heart. The Holy Spirit and even a little sin do not mix. God does not compromise, so you should not either. Seek to reject all the sin in your life, just like you would the teaspoon of bird droppings before they got mixed into the perfect brownie batter.

delight |

What is it about the flesh that makes it hostile to God (v. 7)?

If someone has zero conviction for sin, no repentance, and zero fruit of the Spirit in their lives, regardless of what they say, is he or she saved? What in these verses give you the answer?

display |

On the surface, this last question sounds judgmental. While we cannot look into someone's heart and know if they are in Christ or not, we can look at the fruit of their lives. If a person has no conviction for their sins and bears no fruit of the Spirit's activity in their life, it is safe to assume they do not know Jesus. Jesus changes people. He makes them different from their old way of life.

If you wonder about your salvation because you still have a teaspoon of sin in your life, don't doubt, just repent and ask God to help you turn away from it. The desire not to sin reveals the true condition of your heart much more than the sin that you may still struggle with. You will never be perfect. But if the driving force of your life is to pursue holiness and be like Christ, then you are on track. Rest in that truth. Write the word "Rest" below to remind you.

> Confess whatever teaspoon of sin is in your life. Adapt the opening words of verse 9 into a prayer. "I am not in the flesh, but in the Spirit."

day 29

DOG EAT DOG

discover |

READ GALATIANS 5:13-15.

For you were called to be free, brothers and sisters; only don't use this freedom as an opportunity for the flesh, but serve one another through love. For the whole law is fulfilled in one statement: Love your neighbor as yourself. But if you bite and devour one another, watch out, or you will be consumed by one another.

Have you ever heard the term, "It's a dog eat dog world"? This phrase is a way to describe a viciously competetive environment. Maybe you've experienced this while trying to make a team, or advance a chair in band, or compete for a scholarship. People who are willing to stop at nothing to get what they want are dangerous. The verses for today warn you about this type of behavior. If you will do anything to get what you want, someone else is usually willing to do more. In this arrangement, both end up consuming each other.

Some of Paul's original readers were infected with the idea that Christians needed both Jesus and strict adherence to the Old Testament law to be saved. The reality is that Jesus alone saves us. In this futile dispute, Christians were devouring one another instead of serving one another in the New Testament love that Jesus calls His followers to. The freedom we are called to is not to abuse others, but to serve one another in love. We must bring the desire to get into that dog eat dog situation under control, because it only leaves ruin in its wake.

delight |

How can you keep from being consumed by the "dog eat dog" situations you might find yourself in throughout your life?

What would the ultimate outcome be for this church if they continued biting and devouring one another over this issue (v.15)?

Lift your pastor and leaders up in prayer. Pray for unity in your church.

display |

In Galatians 5:16-26, Paul described the stark differences between the outcomes of a mindset driven by the flesh and a mindset driven by the Spirit. Love for one another, especially in the church, is both an outcome of the Spirit's presence and perfect fulfillment of what Jesus established when He proclaimed the Law fulfilled by our love for God and for one another. If your church is experiencing conflict right now, take a note from one of the first churches of the New Testament and let love and grace win.

If you have lingering tension with someone in your church, let Scripture be the tie-breaker. Own every bit of it that is your fault according to the Bible and make things right. Even if there is no conflict in your ministry (for now), increase the love. By the gifts the Spirit has given you, serve just like this text instructs. Be an active contributor in your church's mission to reach your community and watch the bond of love increase.

The Way Out

FRESH & CLEAN

discover |

READ 1 JOHN 1:9.

If we confess our sins, he is faithful and righteous to forgive us our sins and to cleanse us from all unrighteousness.

Do you remember the colossal messes you made and how unbelievably dirty you would get as a child? Unless you have the unremovable chocolate stain on your face from ten years ago, there has never been a mess that a shower could not clean. There is nothing like that fresh-out-of-the-shower feeling. You feel like a new person. This feeling parallels a spiritual truth. There is never a stain on our souls that God's inexhaustible grace cannot completely wash away.

This unending renewal comes from God's faithfulness to us, not our faithfulness to Him. It flows from His righteousness that will not be emptied, though it forgives a million Christians a minute for a thousand millennia. The word "all" is important. Yes, He has forgiven you even for that sin for which you have not yet forgiven yourself. The Bible says "all," and that means all.

As you have worked through this devotional, you may have felt some discouragement when you came to an area you struggle to have self-control in. Don't be discouraged. Confess it to God and ask Him to help you. And guess what? He will. He loves to show you grace and forgiveness. It is not His desire for you to abuse His grace and forgiveness, but to let what He freely gives change your heart and make you more like Jesus in the process.

delight |

What is the difference between receiving God's grace for your sin and abusing God's grace for your sin?

Describe what it feels like to be cleansed by the faithfulness and righteousness of God.

display |

God is omniscient. Confessing sin to Him is not telling Him something He did not already know. Instead, it brings honesty to your relationship with Him. Your forgiveness was secured upon Christ's crucifixion and resurrection. So, without mistaking His grace for permission to sin, take full advantage of the grace purchased by Jesus on the cross, and confess every time you sin. Do not repeatedly beat yourself up for sin, but believe this verse instead: "As far as the east is from the west, so far has he removed our transgressions from us" (Psalm 103:12).

When you fail at self-control in the future, ask God to forgive you and cleanse you from unrighteousness right away. Give yourself a physical reminder of this verse. Grab a bar of soap and throw it in your purse or backpack. As you smell the soap throughout the day, let it remind you of that fresh and clean feeling you get after a shower, which is a perfect reflection of the forgiveness God offers us through His grace.

Tell God that you believe He is faithful and righteous. Because you believe this and trust Him, confess your sin to Him. Feel the forgiveness.

The Way Out

Walk With Me

WHAT IS ACCOUNTABILITY?

Essentially, being accountable to someone means you have to answer to them. Now, this can sound very formal, strict, or even like this is someone who's over you in a position of authority. While we certainly are accountable to those in authority over us—like parents or guardians, teachers, small group leaders, and pastors—biblical accountability ultimately rests with God. We are accountable to Him for what we do with the life He has given us. However, accountability can also mean giving someone permission to ask us tough questions and walk through God's Word with us—all with the purpose of growing deeper in our faith.

FIND AN ACCOUNTABILITY PARTNER

When we reference accountability in the church, we're often referring to an accountability partner or someone we answer to about spiritual matters, personal struggles, or life in general. While this person cannot command us to act a certain way, we give them permission to ask tough questions that will help us grow in our faith walk.

An accountability partner should always be of the same gender and is typically someone who's on equal standing with you or just a little further along in his or her faith walk. For example, this might be another girl or guy in your small group, the college group, or even the church at large. Usually, however, this is not a person who is in already in authority over you.

Finding an accountability partner isn't something we should take lightly. Rather, this is a process to enter into prayerfully. Ask God who in your life you can trust to help you walk closer to Him and grow in your understanding of His Word. As God directs, seek out this person and ask him or her to pray about becoming your accountability partner. Unless he or she has already been praying about asking you the same, then allow them some time to seek the Lord on this as well. God is the bonding agent of solid relationships, and your spiritual growth is important. While we experience freedom in our relationship with God, we also want to treat it with the reverence, respect, and responsibility it deserves.

How to Build a Relationship with Your Accountability Partner

1. **Begin with prayer.** Thank God for bringing you together. Pray that He will give each of you the strength and courage to ask tough questions. Ask God to soften your heart to receive correction from one another and respond in gentleness when answering a tough question. Pray that you would never sit in a seat of judgment above your friend, but that you would point him or her consistently toward God because of your love for God and that person. Ask God to show you how to encourage and lift one another up, even as you have difficult conversations. Pray that God would give you a close relationship and draw you closer to Him through it.

2. **Consider walking through a Bible study or book of the Bible together, checking in regularly to discuss what God is showing each one of you.** If you walk through a book of the Bible together, don't just read it. Ask yourself important questions about the text. For example, you may choose to summarize the content, determine the teaching about God, and then look at how to apply the teaching to your lives.

3. **Ask Questions.** It can be so intimidating to be open or encourage someone else to be open about their hurts and struggles—even their joys. But accountability doesn't work if we aren't honest with each other. This relationship is a place where you openly share about your struggles and temptations. This is someone who lovingly checks in on you and consistently points you toward making God-honoring choices. Here are some good questions to ask your accountability partner about …

… difficult situations.
How did you do with your _____ assignments this week?
How have you responded when someone yelled at/mistreated/gossiped about you this week?
When you were tempted to _____, what did you do?

… time with God.
Have you prayed about _____ this week?
When have you spent time studying the Bible this week?
How is your Scripture memory going? Would you like to share a verse with me?

... relationships.
How have you handled interactions with _____ this week?
What did you do when you were tempted to push past boundaries with your significant other?
What did you do when you were frustrated/angry/upset about something with your family this week?

... reasons to rejoice.
When has something gone wrong and you've chosen to trust God instead?
What's one new and awesome thing you've learned from your Bible study this week?
How have you seen prayers (yours or those of someone close to you) answered

Your Turn

If you don't have one already, pray about who God might be leading you to ask to be your accountability partner. If you have one already, sit with them and think of what questions you might add to this list.

My Weakness, His Strengths

In the Day 20 Devotion: *Weak Spots*, we learned that to avoid temptation requires us to know our weak spots. While it can be unhealthy to exclusively focus on our weaknesses and failures, it is healthy to acknowledge them and know them well enough to defend against them. Spend some time in prayer, asking the Holy Spirit to guide you as you examine your heart, determining areas of weakness in your life.

In the column labeled, "When I am Weak," write out any personal struggles that come to mind. Then, look to Scripture. Beside each "weakness," in the column labeled, "God is Strong," write out a Scripture that speaks specifically to that weakness or encourages you to be strong. The first is filled in for you as an example.

When I am Weak

I am often tempted to gossip about my friends.

God is Strong

Instead of gossiping, God calls us to speak words that bring life and build up others (Eph 4:29).

notes